Out of Line

Drawings from the Arts Council Collection

Arts Council Collection

Published on the occasion of *Out of Line: Drawings from the Arts Council Collection*, an Arts Council Collection exhibition toured by National Touring Exhibitions from the Hayward Gallery, London, for the Arts Council of England.

Exhibition tour:

| | |
|---|---|
| York City Art Gallery, York | 2 June – 15 July 2001 |
| Glynn Vivian Art Gallery, Swansea | 8 September – 21 October |
| Graves Art Gallery, Sheffield | 27 October – 8 December |
| Oriel Mostyn, Llandudno | 15 December 2001 – 27 January 2002 |
| The Potteries Museum & Art Gallery, Stoke-on-Trent | 2 February – 17 March |
| Middlesbrough Art Gallery, Middlesbrough | 23 March – 12 May |
| Wingfield Arts, Eye | 18 May – 30 June |

Exhibition selected by Suzanne Cotter
Exhibition organized by Suzanne Cotter, assisted by Jessica Fisher

Texts and quotations compiled by Suzanne Cotter and Jessica Fisher: where published sources are not indicated, quotations have been provided directly by the artists for this publication.

Designed by Secondary Modern
Printed in England by The Beacon Press

Front cover: David Shrigley, *'At the earliest point of early morning...'*, 1998 (cat. 53)
Back cover: Craigie Aitchison, *Man Sitting (Yellow)*, 1975 (cat. 2)

Published by Hayward Gallery Publishing, London SE1 8XX, UK

Hayward Gallery Publishing titles are distributed outside North and South America and Canada by Cornerhouse Publications, 70 Oxford Street, Manchester M1 5NH (tel. 0161 200 1503; fax. 0161 237 1504).

For further information about works in the Arts Council Collection, please write to Isobel Johnstone, Curator, Arts Council Collection, Hayward Gallery, Belvedere Road, London SE1 8XX.

## Preface

The Arts Council Collection exists to support and promote the work of living artists in Britain. With more than 7000 paintings, sculptures, photographs, videos and installations, purchased since its foundation in 1946, the Collection is a living document of diverse and changing approaches to artistic practice. It is also the most widely dispersed national loan collection in Britain.

Exhibitions created for the National Touring Exhibitions programme which, like the Arts Council Collection, is managed by the Hayward Gallery on behalf of the Arts Council of England, are an important part of making the Collection visible. Shows may focus on a particular artist or theme; they may also be selected by artists, curators or writers who bring to the Collection very different perspectives. In the light of ongoing interest in the processes and ideas which lie behind an artist's work, and with the current emphasis on drawing in contemporary art, it seems particularly timely to look at some of the drawings which are in the Collection.

*Out of Line* presents more than sixty drawings dating from the 1930s to the present. It includes studies and sketches by many of Britain's most distinguished sculptors and painters, and offers the chance to discover works by artists for whom drawing is their preferred medium. In keeping with the spirit of the Collection, the exhibition does not aim to be exhaustive in its selection but, rather, it makes visible works which are rarely consistently on view for reasons of light sensitivity, and which give an indication of the diverse and changing approaches to this most fundamental of artistic activities.

My thanks go to Hayward Gallery Exhibitions Curator, Suzanne Cotter, who has selected and organized this exhibition, and to Jessica Fisher, who has assisted her in its realization. The Curator of the Collection, Isobel Johnstone, has provided invaluable advice and support for the exhibition in all its aspects, as has Jill Constantine, its Assistant Curator, and the Arts Council Collection team. Geock Brown's patient attention to framing of works in the exhibition has been crucial, as has the technical support of Ryan Rodgers and Richard Nesham. I also wish to thank the Hayward Gallery's Art Publisher, Linda Schofield, and our Publishing Coordinator, Caroline Wetherilt, for their work and skilful attention to every detail in producing this publication. I extend my thanks as well to our Education Programmer, Helen Luckett, for producing contextual material for visitors to the exhibition. Finally, but not least, I would like to express my appreciation to the artists represented, for the contributions many of them have made to this publication, and especially for their work, without which this exhibition would not be possible.

Susan Ferleger Brades
Director, Hayward Gallery

# Contents

# Out of Line: A Study of Sorts
## Suzanne Cotter

Drawings are generally considered to be an artist's most intimate works. Traditionally associated with the first step towards the creation of a painting or sculpture, drawing also serves as a means for remembering things seen, or for giving form to more abstract ideas. Some artists make independent drawings as a parallel practice to works in different media, whilst others use drawing as their main form of expression. Many artists today use drawing as one of a number of possible ways in which they might choose to make work. In all of these cases, the physical directness of drawing, its economy, its association with creative process, and its traditionally ambiguous position within the fine arts as being both fundamental and marginal to the so-called 'completed work', are qualities which are prized and exploited.

Many of the early drawings in the Arts Council Collection are studies. Some are student sketches, most, however, are the result of a process of elaboration of a particular motif or idea towards a subsequent work in painting or sculpture. Their subject matter ranges from the descriptive to the abstract. Some are small in format, on pages from the artists' sketchbooks, and are of simple and apparently rapid execution. Several bear annotations: reminders of things seen, or indications of things to try next. They all reveal to some extent a process of analysis, distillation and synthesis into a graphic form. Individually, they offer insight into a particular artist's practice. Together, they reveal a rich diversity of approach.

Drawing's potential for reducing complex visual sensations to essential relationships is most evident in the study. In his pencil drawings of bones and shells (cat. 37-40), Henry Moore concentrated on the effects of natural forces on their curving forms. Ben Nicholson's simple line drawings of the landscape (cat. 41) are a kind of 'meditation' on the nature of form at its most essential. Unlike Nicholson or Moore, who used drawing as a tool to explore particular formal qualities, Graham Sutherland noted very specific aspects of nature, such as the sharp contours of a palm leaf (cat. 57), which he could develop as expressive devices in his paintings. Whilst William Coldstream was rigorously applying his system of proportion to studies such as *Temporary Bridge over the Volturno, Capua,* 1944 (cat. 13), his friend and co-founder of the Euston School of Painting in the 1940s, Victor Pasmore, began with the simplest elements – the straight line and the curve – from which a referential image developed (cat. 46). This interrelation between the descriptive and the abstract which the act of drawing encompasses is particularly developed in the studies of Bridget Riley for whom the lessons of 'pictorial organization' and 'structure', learnt in her early life drawing classes, were fundamental to her enquiries into abstract painting (cat. 50).

At its most pared down, a drawing is an arrangement of lines; the page its space. At its most elaborate, it is a complex application of styles, shading, tones and colour. The organization of lines in sculptor William Tucker's

*Tunnel* drawings, 1975 (cat. 58-61) articulates a dynamic space within the imaginary field of the paper. In contrast, the contours of Craigie Aitchison's crayon drawing (cat. 2) seem to absorb the surrounding space of the page, and impart a sense of frailty and introspection to the seated, nude figure. L.S. Lowry captured the character of his anonymous *Woman with Long Hair,* 1964 (cat. 33) with a series of rapidly executed pencil strokes. Richard Hamilton, on the other hand, made his colour pencil study *Swingeing London,* 1968 (cat. 20) as part of a sophisticated process involving multiple works and the pre-existing source of the newspaper photograph. Maintaining the cropped frame of the original image for his drawing, Hamilton concentrated on the most telling items of his pictorial narrative: the cuffs, the hands shielding the faces of the square-jawed Robert Fraser (Hamilton's dealer at the time) and the full-lipped rock star Mick Jagger.

Artists are constantly exploring the possibilities offered by a given medium. With painting, it might be the use of colour and tone, the application of paint as a thin layer or as a thick surface, the use of a controlled or an expressive brushstroke, in making a representational or abstract composition; with video, it might be movement, framing, camera angles, and the editing process which are all taken into account as elements to play with. This experimentation applies equally to drawing in the ways artists mine the possibilities offered by different materials, techniques and graphic styles according to their own interests and preoccupations.

Nigel Hall is a sculptor who also makes drawings. His *Untitled Drawing,* 1972 (cat. 17) does not relate to a three-dimensional work but his use of charcoal, applied in heavy, directional strokes, and cut through with fine rectilinear incisions, implies a palpable physical presence. Carl Plackman also makes sculptures alongside his drawings (cat. 49), however his objects, which are part-real and part-imagined, and drawn in light pencil, do not so much occupy space as float in a cloud of poetic suggestion. Douglas Binder's drawings are graphic alternatives to sculpture in which he has played on the co-existent precision and furriness of the lines of his felt pen to create strangely monumental yet illusory landscapes and architectures (cat. 7, 8). In the case of painters Frank Auerbach and Maggie Hambling, their gestural use of charcoal and ink is less about creating a tangible form than it is about making visible the traces of physical engagement of the artist with his or her subject. This directness of the graphic mark translates also into the untrammelled, spontaneous expression of Turi Werkner's 'psychedelic' *MM33,* 1976 (cat. 64).

Drawing is the trace of an activity. For some artists, the process of making a work is as important as the end result. David Connearn is interested in the act of drawing at its most elemental: his emotional state on a given day, the lightness or heaviness of his touch, the temperature and the humidity effecting the paper. His large-scale pen and pencil drawings are a seismographic map of the artist's accumulation over time of row after row of tightly-spaced horizontal lines building up a dense field of gently vibrating fluctuations (cat. 14). Emma Kay refers less to the physical conditions of drawing than to its capacity to translate the act of remembering. Her series of maps of the world drawn from memory (cat. 28), intricately outlined in pencil and neatly annotated with the names of capital cities and major rivers, reveals her personal geography of the world as experienced through a combination of education and lived experience. In Rachel Lowe's video, *A Letter to an Unknown Person, No. 5,* 1998 (cat. 32), the act of drawing becomes a metaphor for time and the impossibility of capturing a particular moment as the artist's attempts to trace the landscape on the window of a moving car result in an incomprehensible tangle of lines.

For contemporary artists who are making drawings, a play on graphic styles – both past and present – and their associations with a particular context, count among their resources. Simon Periton appropriates the language of Victorian decoration and military insignia with his paper cut-out 'doilies' to comment on the fragility and transience of cultural attitudes. Keith Tyson adopts the diagrammatic language of a scientist scribbling furiously on his blackboard wall drawings (cat. 62) to illustrate the interconnectedness of his practice in which he generates works in every conceivable medium, from painting and sculpture to photography and performance. While Richard Hamilton and Allen Jones (cat. 27) in the 1960s worked with popular imagery from advertising, newspapers and magazines, younger artists Jim Medway, Adam Dant and David Shrigley exploit the language of comic strips, graffiti, telephone doodles and children's book illustrations. If they owe a certain allegiance to Glen Baxter's 'Boys Own'-style captioned vignettes (cat. 4), and to David Hockney's child-like rendering in his works of the 1960s and '70s (cat. 22-24), the apparent naïveté of David Shrigley's notebook-sized drawings also contrasts with the increasingly saturated and sophisticated image culture of contemporary life. In this context, the hand-made, the technically impoverished, and the banality of everyday experiences become expressions of unmediated truths.

Faced with the diversity of works in the Collection, it is interesting to consider the ways in which earlier attitudes and approaches to drawing resonate and are transformed by younger generations. The legacy of 1970s conceptualism with its emphasis on language, process and duration, evident in Roger Ackling's *Five hour cloud drawing,* 1980 (cat. 1), is recognizable in Graham Gussin's translation of a recorded conversation into a three-dimensional waveform (cat. 16). David Hockney's sketches appear pivotal to more contemporary artists' use of stylistic and pictorial quotation. In his coloured drawing *French Shop,* 1971 (cat. 23), Hockney flouts traditional conventions of academic draughtsmanship by placing a roughly-shaded pitched roof house, complete with smoking chimney, within a framework of squared lines. Eduardo Paolozzi's studies of figures from Rembrandt (cat. 44) and African carvings (cat. 45), which he made in Oxford in the mid-1940s while a student at the Ruskin School, also strike a contemporary chord in the visual language of Michael Landy's *Scrapheap Services,* 1995 (cat. 30). Whilst Landy's ink drawing covers every square inch of the paper with a plethora of signs, symbols and images which chart the production and recycling of waste, Paolozzi's technically skilled drawings of two disparate subjects – European painting and non-western statuary – appear less as traditional studies than as elements of a vast image bank without hierarchy.

In a recent interview, the American sculptor Richard Serra summed up the relevance of drawing within changing artistic contexts: 'Certain aspects of how to draw have been lost over the centuries because it is not as relevant an occupation as it was for artists in the past. Géricault could draw a horse jumping out of a barn on fire; that facility has been lost. On the other hand, artists have learned to draw in other ways to concretize their experience.'* Artists will always value drawing. They will continue also to find new ways to adapt drawing to their own ends. It is this capacity for reinvigoration which ensures that drawing will always be important and endlessly interesting.

* R. Eric Davis, 'Richard Serra Talks About Drawing', in *Art on Paper*, May-June 2000

**Further Reading**

*Paul Klee Notebooks Volume 1: The Thinking Eye,* Lund Humphries, London, 1973

P. Rawson, *Seeing through Drawing,* British Broadcasting Corporation, London, 1979

*Hayward Annual 1982: British Drawing,* Arts Council of Great Britain, London, 1982

Deanna Petherbridge, *The Primacy of Drawing: An Artist's View,* The South Bank Centre, London, 1991

*The Body of Drawing: Drawings by Sculptors,* The South Bank Centre, London, 1993

Michael Craig-Martin, *Drawing the Line: Reappraising drawing past and present,* The South Bank Centre, London, 1995

*From Figure to Object: A Century of Sculptor's Drawings,* Frith Street Gallery, and Karsten Schubert, London, 1996

Cornelia H. Butler, *After Image: Drawing through Process,* The Museum of Contemporary Art, Los Angeles, 1999

# Artists' Works and Texts

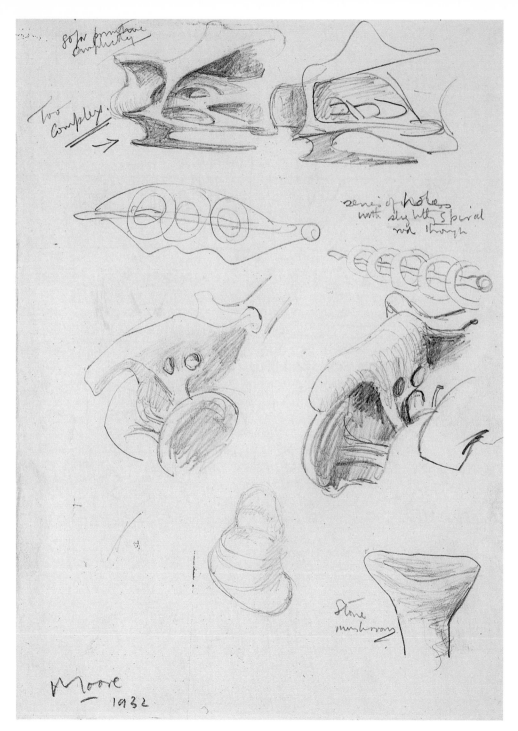

**39** *Studies and Transformations of Bones of Shells and Mushrooms* 1932

# Henry Moore

The human figure is what interests me most deeply, but I have found principles of form and rhythm from the study of natural objects such as pebbles, rocks, bones, trees, plants, etc. Pebbles and rocks show nature's way of working stone. Smooth, sea-worn pebbles show the wearing away, rubbed treatment of stone and the principle of asymmetry. Rocks show the hacked, hewn treatment of stone, and have a jagged nervous block rhythm.

Bones have a marvellous structural strength and hard tenseness of form, subtle transition of one shape into the next and great variety in section. Shells show nature's hard but hollow form (metal sculpture) and have a wonderful completeness of single shape.

Henry Moore in Philip James (ed.), *Henry Moore on Sculpture*, London, 1966, p. 70 reprinted in Alan G. Wilkinson, *The Drawings of Henry Moore*, Tate Gallery, London, 1977, p. 24

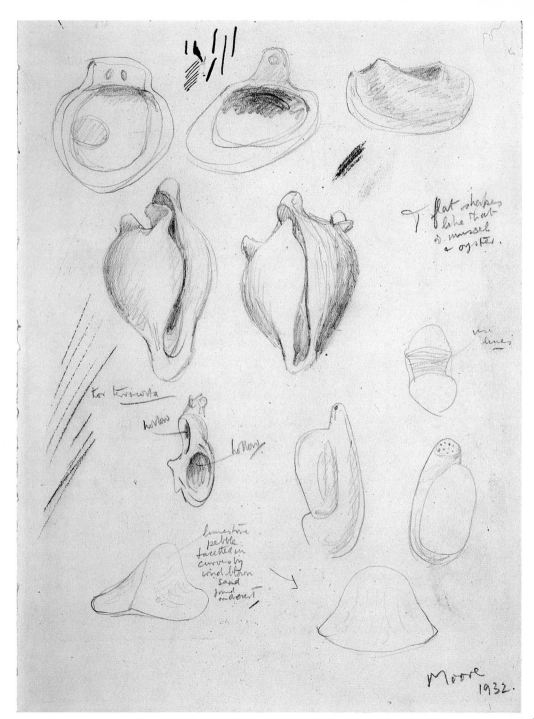

**40** *Studies of Shells and Pebbles* 1932

**13** *Temporary Bridge over the Volturno, Capua* 1944

## William Coldstream

One of the things with which I had tremendous difficulty at the Slade was doing a representation of anything. I found that, whereas most of the students really could do what seemed to be magical drawings, which may not be very nice to look at but seem to be exactly like the model, my things looked absolutely ridiculous and sort of childish. And after I left the Slade, I determined [...] that I would learn to draw things which it had never occurred to me to set myself to do.

William Coldstream in David Sylvester, 'An Unpublished Interview', 1962 in *The Paintings of William Coldstream,1908–1987,* Tate Gallery, London, 1990, p. 27

## Victor Pasmore

What I have done [...] is not the
result of a process of abstraction in
front of nature, but a method of
construction emanating from within. I
have tried to compose as music is
composed, with formal elements
which, in themselves, have no
descriptive qualities at all [...]. That
ancient maxim, 'art imitates nature',
must no longer be construed in the
superficial sense which the schools
and academies of visual painting
have imposed upon it, but in its
deeper meaning – art imitates nature
in its manner of operation.

*Victor Pasmore,* The Arts Council of Great Britain,
London, 1980, p. 10

**46** *Beach in Cornwall* 1950

**41** *Cloisters, San Gimignano* 1950

## Ben Nicholson

When you draw something that's already a work of art, it sets a special problem. But you really get to know the spirit of a place that way – there's a big difference between merely looking at a building and living with it for two or three hours (or for a couple of centuries) while making a drawing. When I draw one of those pieces of Greek and Italian architecture, I am, I suppose, drawing the form. But it's the spirit of the architecture that I look at, not its stones.

'The Life and Opinions of an English 'Modern':
In Conversation with Vera and John Russell' in
*Weekly Review*, p. 28, *The Sunday Times*,
28 April 1963

In some moods one cannot put a foot right and in others not a foot wrong. […] It is not the drawing that is difficult but finding and recognising the mood. When in this right mood one knows well that something will come.

*Ben Nicholson: New Works*, Galerie Beyeler, Basel,
May-June 1973

**31** *Landscape Drawing, Wiltshire Downs* 1966

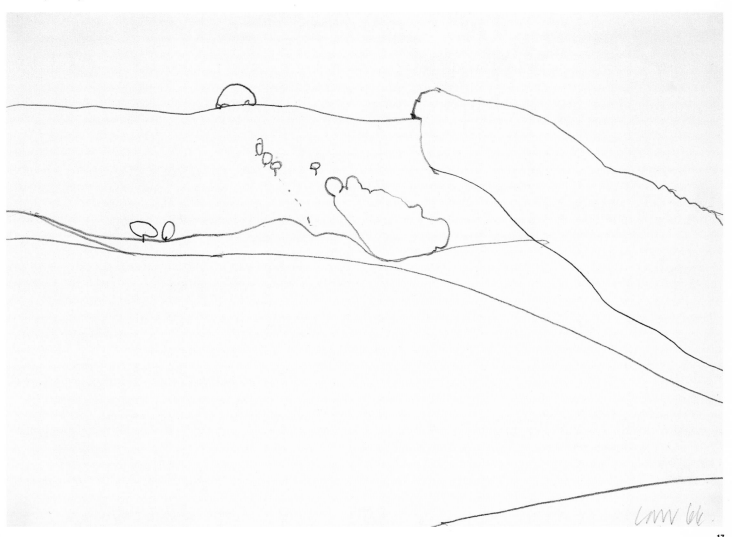

**36** *Bath c.*1953

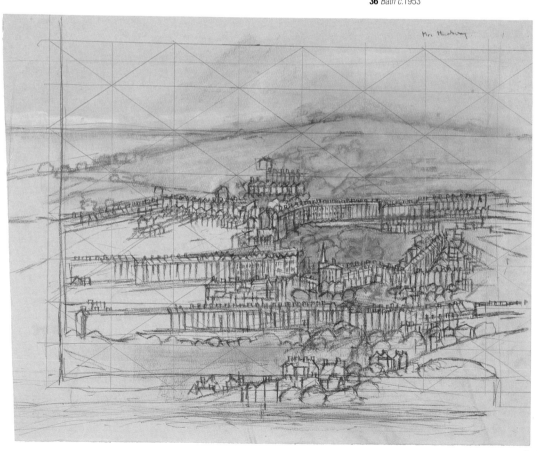

## David Hockney

Drawing is everywhere in David Hockney's work [...] it forms a continuous activity. [...] He may draw out of his head, from nature or from photographs of all kinds: postcards, book illustrations, photographs in magazines and advertisements. [...] If he is using photographs he tends to make a drawing first to simplify the image. For complex paintings such as his big double portraits he has found photographs do not give enough information, 'You have to draw and make notes'. All kinds of drawings can be involved in a painting from a quick sketch out of his head, the start of a compositional idea, to squared up drawings for enlargement and detailed studies from nature. Although he has said he does not pay much attention to the drawings themselves while painting, he may make more drawings while a picture is in progress.

Joanna Drew, *Drawing towards Painting 2,* The Arts Council of Great Britain, London, 1967

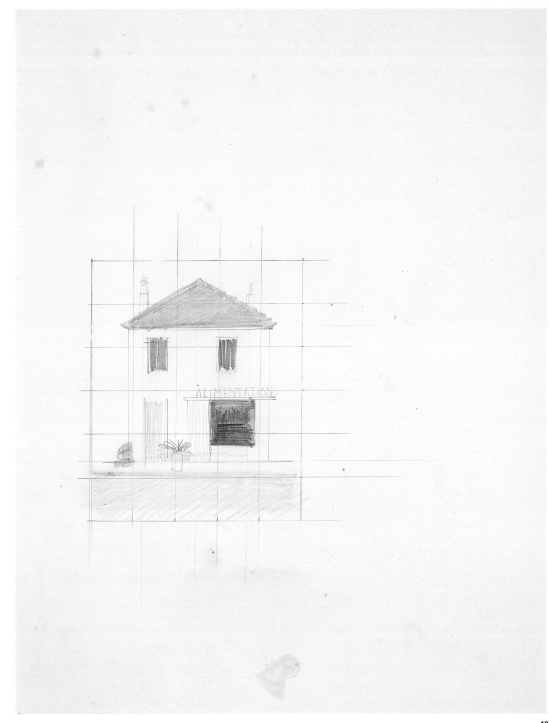

**23** *French Shop* 1971

**Allen Jones**

His sketchbooks form a diary of pictorial ideas [...]. He also makes sketchbook drawings 'to shift inertia' when he has become 'stuck with an image' or has been working on it too long. In this situation he finds 'the only way is to draw fairly rapidly until one realises oneself'. He also draws when at a loss for ideas or to loosen up ideas, and very often when 'trying to find the right level where a thing exists without becoming a fragment' or 'until a new slant or nuance comes up which wasn't preconceived'.

Joanna Drew, *Drawing towards Painting 2,*
The Arts Council of Great Britain, London, 1967

**27** *Sheet of drawings for Shoe Wheel* 1965-66

## Bridget Riley

At Goldsmiths' School of Art I met a marvellous teacher who taught me drawing. His name was Sam Rabin. In those days you still were taught drawing. I was there when the class began and when it ended. For three years I drew day and night. Without realising it I absorbed, through the techniques of life drawing, many important things such as pictorial organisation, structure and the stripping away of the visual image to see what's beneath. For example, when I had started to draw, Sam Rabin would come up and say, 'What's the model doing, sitting or standing? Is your drawing standing?' He taught me to order my work, to develop it in methodical stages, to see a thing as a whole, not in parts. He stressed the importance of the relationship between things; how everything matters; what to expect of yourself; how to make an advance and consolidate it; then make another advance – and not to expect advance after advance; how to raise the level of work slowly. That was gold – and something I have kept with me.

Robert Kudielka (ed.), *The Eye's Mind: Bridget Riley, Collected Writings 1965-1999*, Thames & Hudson, London, 1999, p. 24

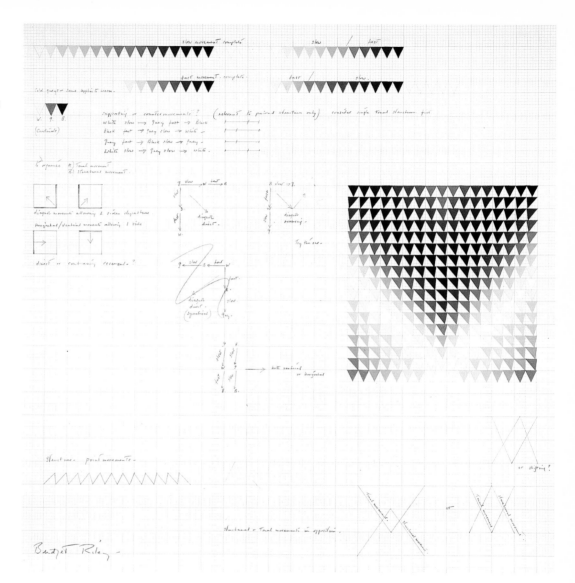

**50** *Structural and Tonal Movements in Opposition* 1966

**63** *Figure in Profile* 1974

## Maggi Hambling

Drawing is the basis of everything I do. It is equal to my paintings and sculpture.

Drawing is like handwriting. It is the most intimate and immediate. This has to do with the simple fact of picking up a piece of charcoal or graphite; it is just the paper, the instrument, and the simultaneous action of the hand and the eye. You have to use your whole body. The touch of whatever instrument you're using is crucial. It's a physical thing. I always think of the piece of paper as the space which the subject inhabits. Every mark that I make must be dictated by the subject.

Maggi Hambling in conversation with Suzanne Cotter, February 2001

**18** *Drawing from Life: Model in a Studio* 1966

**2** *Man Sitting (Yellow)* 1975

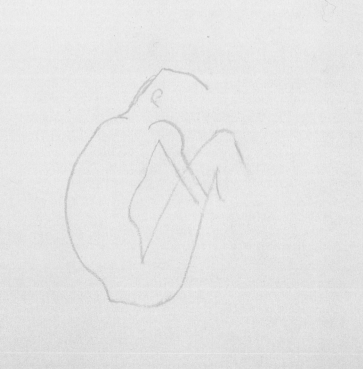

## William Tucker

Construction enabled me to strip away an old image of the body and an old approach to modelling. In a way those years were like a prolonged anatomy lesson, analysing the bones before adding the flesh.

*William Tucker: The Philosophers, Sculpture and Drawings 1989-1992*, Maak Gallery, London, 1993

**59** *'T (Tunnel)' — Tii* 1975

## L.S. Lowry

My characters? They are all people you might see in a park. They are real people, sad people; something's gone wrong in their lives. I'm attracted to sadness, and there are some very sad things you see. There is something about these people that is remarkable, you know. They have a look in their eye. You wonder what they are really looking at. There is a mystery about them. I feel I am compelled to try and draw them. I wonder all the time: what is their life?

L.S. Lowry in Edwin Mullins, 'The Lonely Life of L.S. Lowry' in Michael Leber and Judith Sandling (eds), *L.S. Lowry,* Phaidon Press and Salford Art Gallery, 1987, p. 81

**33** *Woman with Long Hair* 1964

## Richard Hamilton

Sometimes things labelled 'drawing' have little to do with overt handling of a medium. It can be that a working drawing is no more than a photograph retouched, or otherwise modified, to lead to further progress of a painting. I would be loath to make a distinction between these and a watercolor or pastel drawing of a more conventional kind.

*Richard Hamilton: Prints, multiples and drawings,* Whitworth Art Gallery, Manchester, 1972, p. 30 reprinted in *Richard Hamilton,* Solomon R. Guggenheim Foundation, New York, 1973, p. 17

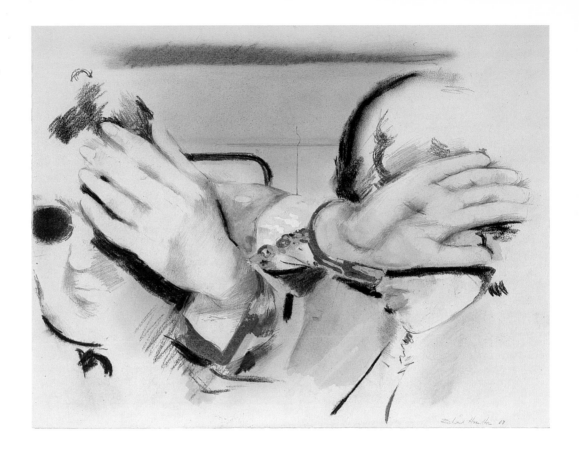

**20** *Swingeing London* 1968

**3** *Head of Brigid* 1973-74.

## Frank Auerbach

Drawing is not a mysterious activity. Drawing is making an image which expresses commitment and involvement. This only comes about after seemingly endless activity before the model or subject, rejecting time and time again ideas which are possible to preconceive. And, whether by scraping off or by rubbing down, it is always beginning again, making new images, destroying images that lie, discarding images that are dead. The only true guide in this search is the special relationship the artist has with the person or landscape from which he is working. Finally, in spite of all this activity of absorption and internalisation the images emerge in an atmosphere of freedom. This is the nature of true draughtsmanship and it is out of this spirit that the paintings of Frank Auerbach grow, glimmering towards the light.

Leon Kossoff, 'The paintings of Frank Auerbach' in *Frank Auerbach,* The Arts Council of Great Britain, London, 1978, p. 9

## Tony Bevan

Each piece of charcoal, whether it be made of willow, poplar or vine, has its own particular qualities, and each piece behaves in its own way. It is unpredictable, shattering and leaving debris.

Tony Bevan, February 2001

**6** *Portrait of a Martyr* 1982

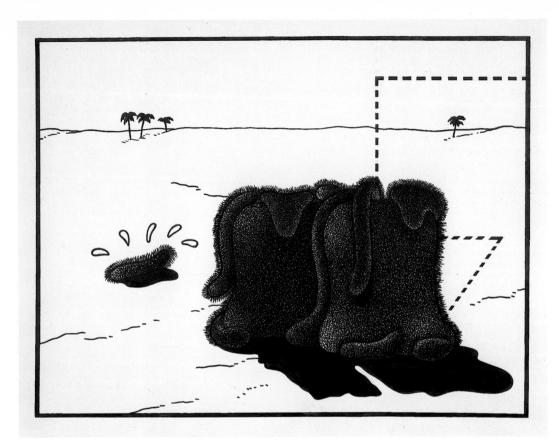

**7** *Desert Incident* 1969

### Douglas Binder

My paintings and drawings have always depicted solid form in conventional space. Too lazy to make sculpture, I make the illusion.
Being bankrupt at the time (1969) my production was limited to drawing and my reading habits limited to *The Beano*. I admired the comic's graphic conventions, which I adapted to my own ends. I wanted to project an enigmatic feel to the drawing, with an implied narrative combined with humour. My influences would seem to lie outside the fine art area although my development led me towards a great interest in De Chirico.

Douglas Binder, March 2001

## Carl Plackman

A drawing is the writing on the wall.
A drawing makes sense out of
nonsense and nonsense out of sense.
A drawing contains more time than it
takes to look at it.
A drawing is a history of experience
and its content is non-visual.
A drawing is never non-referential; a
drawing is a way of thinking.
A drawing is a means of searching
for identity.
A drawing is sometimes the catalyst,
sometimes assistant and sometimes
the critic.
A drawing's space can be finite and it
can be limitless.
A drawing's content is never wholly
contained in the drawing.
A drawing is always made by
somebody.

Carl Plackman, artist's notes, 1972

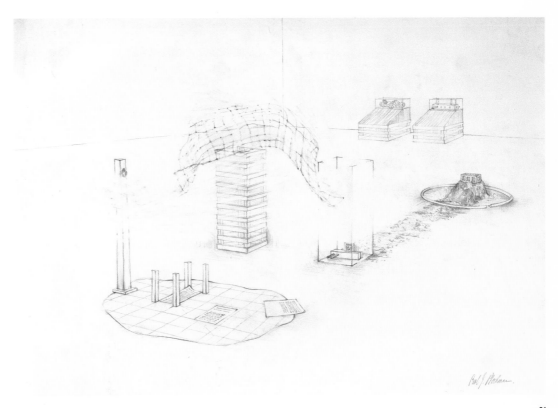

**49** *Untitled Drawing ("Net")* 1969

**17** *Untitled Drawing* 1972

## Nigel Hall

At the end of the sixties, I felt […] a need to draw in a different way, to make the drawings a strong physical fact in their own right and I found the means of doing this with charcoal. I use it in layer upon layer to build up a rich density of black, with the pure white of the paper piercing through, from the finest white line to larger areas. I also wanted to make a modulation from the extremes of black and white through using charcoal dust, formed in the act of drawing, and fixed at each stage. I was interested in progressions and intervals and reversals of black and white to show the way in which an image can dominate or be submerged by its context.

*Nigel Hall: early work with sculpture and drawings 1965-1980,* Warwick Gallery, London, 22 May-11 July 1980

## David Connearn

I made *Coming-Going* over a period
of two months. The work's
appearance and dimensions are
directly related to my body: It was
drawn line below line, from the extent
of the reach of my left hand to the
extent of my reach on the right. The
nature of the line changes as the pen
moves towards the centre, changes
hands, and then moves away again. It
traces the contingency within which
attention, intention and effort become
manifest. The work is a meditation on
the ways and means with which we
represent presence, on control and
uncontrollability and on an underlying
texture of reality which permeates
these conventions.

David Connearn, March 2001

**14** *Coming-going* 1987

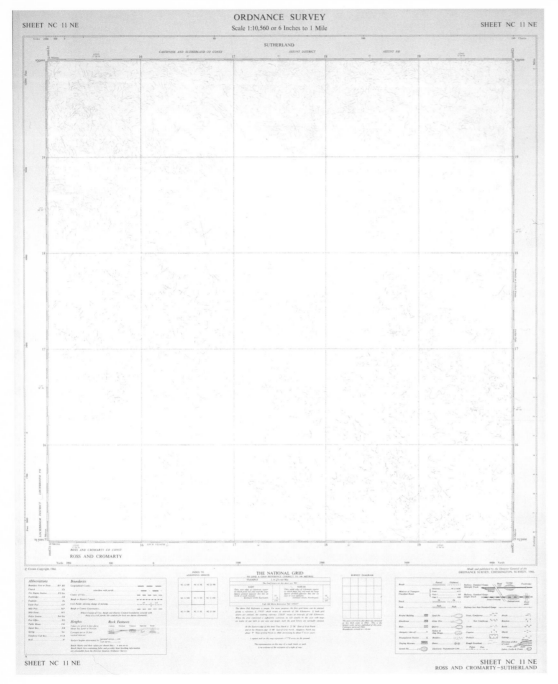

## Tony Carter

Drawing is largely a speculative activity for me and, more often than not, an aid to visualizing the objects I make. It is usually diagrammatic in format and improvised on a small scale in the notebooks that I almost always carry with me.

Sometimes these 'diagrams' extend beyond the technical and speculative to serve a meditative purpose. [...] *Remembering Landscape* was conceived at the outset as being about this meditative state.

Tony Carter, February 2001

**11** *Remembering Landscape* 1974-77

## Turi Werkner

Turi Werkner […] covers enormous
sheets of paper or transparent
celluloid with obsessive incessant
doodling varying between whorls, so
compact and systematic as to create
an almost matt surface, and a free-
ranging line changing direction and
strength so often as to suggest life
under the microscope or among
grass-roots. Werkner is a true
automatist. His hand is at the service
of his imagination. Every mark he
makes shows a conviction unaffected
by the intervention of conscious
control. He is the spectator of his
own creative process.

George Melly, …*a cold wind brushing the temple:
An exhibition of drawing, painting and sculpture
purchased by George Melly for the Arts Council
Collection,* The Arts Council of Great Britain,
London, 1979

**64** *MM33* 1976

## Rachel Lowe

The film documents my attempt to draw with a black marker pen onto the window of a moving car, the landscape, as it flies past. Depicting only my hand, the pen and the landscape, the piece is fundamentally concerned with our need or desire to capture a particular moment in time, the impossibility of ever adequately doing so, and the resultant sense of loss. The futility inherent within the title becomes apparent in the drawing, as the failure of my hand to keep up results in an increasingly incomprehensible mass of black lines, their confusion rather than clarity acting as the defining emotion of the piece of work.

Rachel Lowe, March 2001

**32** *A Letter to an Unknown Person, No. 5* 1998

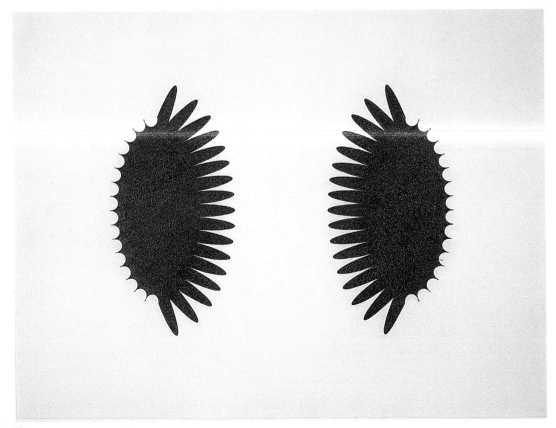

**21** *Untitled Drawing (3)* 1998-99

## Keith Tyson

There can be other ways of drawing,
we don't exist in isolation, often a
work is simply argued into existence.

Keith Tyson, *One of Each: a small volume of
experiments,* Galerie Krinzinger Wien, 2000, p. 36

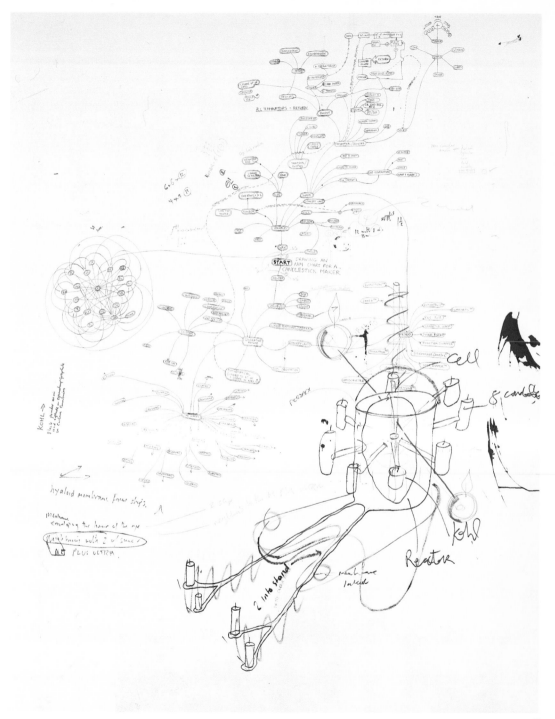

**62** *Applied Art Machine Chart: Candlestick
Maker* 1999

**34** *Winter Bouquet* 1947

## Simon Periton

Any drawing that I might do is usually done with a scalpel cutting through the surface of the paper rather than making a mark with a pencil on it. A pencil line can always be erased but a knife cut has a certainty that appeals to me. In a way, it is like making a series of medical incisions. Cutting away creates the picture, leaving something fragile which barely holds together. My work is more quartered than drawn.

Simon Periton, March 2001

**47** *SP* 1995

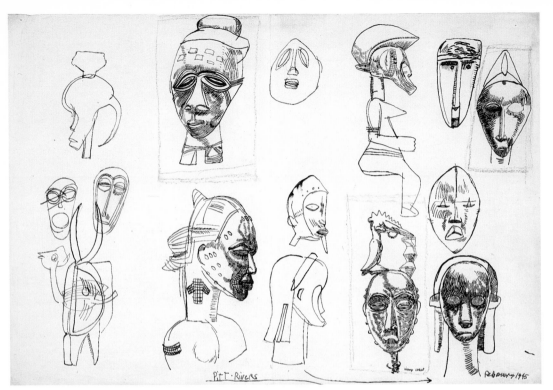

**45** *Pitt-Rivers* 1945

## Eduardo Paolozzi

[…] drawing in the Life Room at the Ruskin seemed a pointless exercise. The only available model […] had to come up from London. With the evacuation of all art schools from London, models had become rare. […] The drawings of my fellow students confirmed my view that drawing something somewhere else had more appeal.

In this strange community, I would depart, probably to the glorious library of the Ashmolean to copy Dürer or Rembrandt facsimiles or, bearing in mind the strange hours of that most wonderful museum, the Pitt Rivers Collection, to study and draw African masks and sculptures.

Eduardo Paolozzi, 'Memoirs', 1994 in Robin Spencer (ed.), *Eduardo Paolozzi. Writings and Interviews*, Oxford University Press, 2000, pp. 55-56

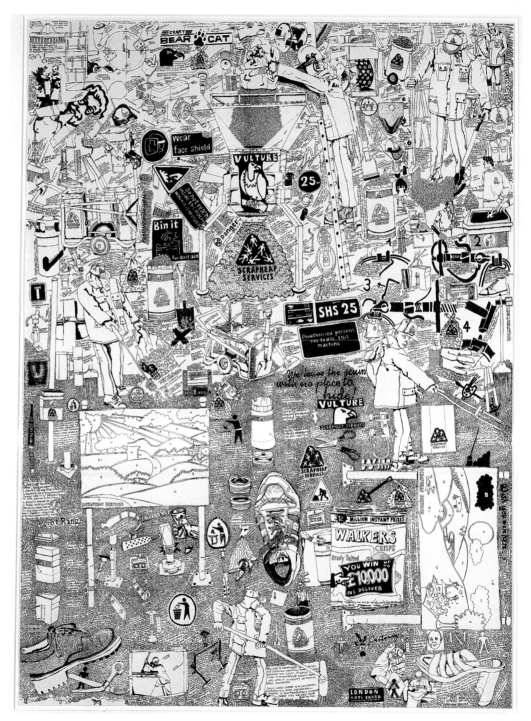

**30** *Scrapheap Services* 1995

Drawing is a form of electricity connecting one thing to another sometimes, and hopefully, in surprising ways. I've always had a soft spot for really bad drawing, the sketches of Giorgio De Chirico, and the sublime images in *Nouvelles Impressions d'Afrique* conjured up by Henri Zo, as commanded (via a detective agency) by the impeccable Raymond Roussel.

Glen Baxter, March 2001

IT SEEMED REX WAS GOING THROUGH A PERIOD OF "FIGURATION"....

**4** *It seemed Rex was going through a period of "figuration"...* 1978

# Adam Dant

As with many other large-scale drawings I have been making over the last four years, this drawing also displays a narrative which is speculative or implied, rather than illustrating a linear scheme of events. In this piece, the usual action that fills each frame is replaced by fictitious names of supposedly emotionally developed characters, whose identities are carried in their peculiar sounding monikers. In the same way that drawing exists as a form of language which is interpreted, or 'read', with a certain amount of subjective response, so

it is in the 'roll call' in this particular drawing that I wanted to have the same resonance in the sound, length, and association of each name as exists in the play of the descriptive line in my other narrative drawings.

The names are all written in the same script, on panels fixed at different heights, to poles stuck into lumps of earth as a type of textual herd. The nature of the names as peculiar and referring to real objects, reflects a compulsive Tourettic use of speech and language that forces

the construction of an image for each, in much the same way that cartoon characters often have aspects of their personality contained in their names (Daffy Duck, Pepe le Pew, Secret Squirrel, Foghorn Leghorn, et al.). In short, it is a 'funny sounding' picture.

Adam Dant, February 2001

**15** *Untitled 2 (Sea of Names)* 1996

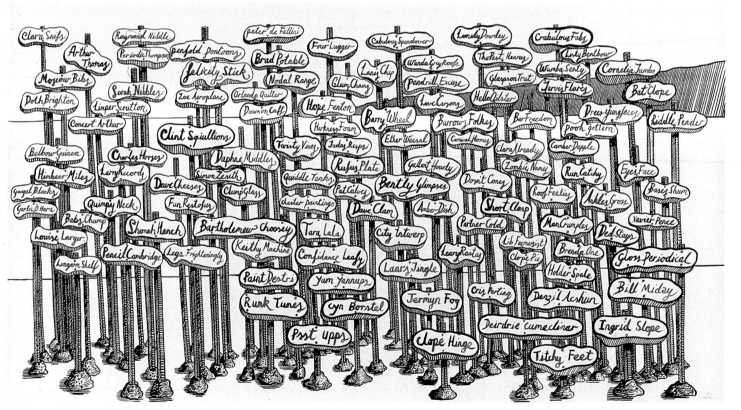

**22** *Fred and Marcia Weisman* 1968

**Jim Medway**

Children's books taught me what to draw and how to draw it. Combined with observations of what surrounds me and the idea of 'gritty' truths, a kind of magic social realism is created.

Jim Medway, March 2001

**35** *Shoe Shop* 1999

10  *A Country Walk* 1980

# David Shrigley

To call Shrigley's drawing style anything in particular would be a mistake. Despite the apparent objectifications they deal with, these are not, in fact, drawings of things at all; rather, they are drawings of the shapes that things, people, ideas and emotions make in our lives. I'm not even sure that it would be altogether accurate to call these works drawings at all.

Will Self, *Why we got the sack from the Museum*, The Redstone Press, London, 1998

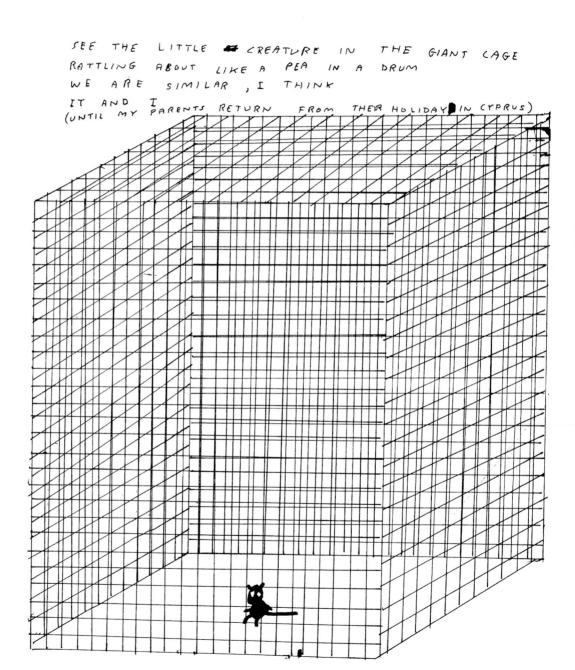

SEE THE LITTLE ☙ CREATURE IN THE GIANT CAGE RATTLING ABOUT LIKE A PEA IN A DRUM WE ARE SIMILAR , I THINK IT AND I (UNTIL MY PARENTS RETURN FROM THEIR HOLIDAY IN CYPRUS)

**55** *'See the little creature in the giant cage...'* 1998

COMPARE OUR PRICES AGAINST OUR COMPETITORS' PRICES

BAKED BEANS! BAKED BEANS! BAKED BEANS! BAKED BEANS! BAKED BEANS! BAKED BEANS!

**54** *'Compare our prices against our competitiors...'* 1998

## Jason Coburn

*Push the Button,* 1996, is from a series of drawings using black ink on Ministry of Defence headed paper. Firstly brushing a wash over the paper, then writing onto it, provides a powerful typographic take on the words depicted. There is a conflicting play between the words and the paper they are scrawled onto. What you are left with is an ambivalent image. The drawings have a sense of doubt, anxiety and disquieting uncertainty.

Jason Coburn, March 2001

**MINISTRY OF DEFENCE**
Main Building, Whitehall, London SW1A 2HB
Telephone (Direct Dialling) 071-21-8
(Switchboard) 071-21-89000

100% Recycled Paper

**12** *Push the Button* 1996

# List of Works

Page references refer to illustrations within this book

**1** (p. 35)
Roger Ackling
(b. 1947, London, UK)
*Five hour cloud drawing* 1980
sunlight on cardboard
62.4 x 75.2 cm
purchased 1981

**2** (p. 24)
Craigie Aitchison
(b. 1926, Edinburgh, UK)
*Man Sitting (Yellow)* 1975
oil pastel on paper
36 x 49 cm
purchased 1975

**3** (p. 28)
Frank Auerbach
(b. 1931, Berlin, Germany)
*Head of Brigid* 1973-74
charcoal on paper
56.3 x 77.5 cm
purchased 1975

**4** (p. 46)
Glen Baxter (b. 1944, Leeds, UK)
*It seemed Rex was going through a period of "figuration"...* 1978
ink on paper
32 x 22.8 cm
purchased 1979
© Glen Baxter

**5**
Glen Baxter
*The Beaker, Hull* 1978
watercolour on paper
34.1 x 49.3 cm
purchased 1979

**6** (p. 29)
Tony Bevan
(b. 1951, Bradford, UK)
*Portrait of a Martyr* 1982
dry pigment, PVA and charcoal
on Triwall
190 x 114 cm
purchased 1982

**7** (p. 30)
Douglas Binder
(b. 1941, Bradford, UK)
*Desert Incident* 1969
indian ink on paper
38.1 x 50.8 cm
purchased 1970

**8**
Douglas Binder
*Procession* 1969
indian ink on paper
38.1 x 50.8 cm
purchased 1970

**9**
Paul Butler
(b. 1947, Bristol, UK)
*Interview* 1979
charcoal, pencil and indian ink
on paper
137 x 91 cm
purchased 1980

**10** (p. 50)
Ian Cameron
(b. 1947, Hampshire, UK)
*A Country Walk* 1980
charcoal, pastel, pencil, felt pen
and collage on paper
40 x 84 cm
purchased 1980

**11** (p. 34)
Tony Carter
(b. 1943, West Riding, UK)
*Remembering Landscape* 1974-77
pencil on gouache on Ordnance
Survey map
65.3 x 53.6 cm
purchased 1982

**12** (p. 53)
Jason Coburn
(b. 1969, Manchester, UK)
*Push the Button* 1996
ink on paper
29.8 x 21 cm
purchased 1997

**13** (p. 14)
William Coldstream
(b. 1908, Belford, UK – d. 1987)
*Temporary Bridge over the Volturno,
Capua* 1944
pencil on paper
22.6 x 13.8 cm
purchased 1977
© Courtesy of the artist's estate/
Bridgeman Art Library

**14** (p. 33)
David Connearn
(b. 1952, Rosendale, UK)
*Coming-going* 1987
ink on paper
203 x 203 cm
purchased 1994

**15** (p. 47)
Adam Dant
(b. 1967, The Fens, UK)
*'Untitled 2' (Sea of Names)* 1996
ink drawing
131.4 x 236 cm
purchased 1997

**16** (p. 36)
Graham Gussin
(b. 1960, London, UK)
*Porno Landscape* 1996
pencil on paper
63.3 x 89.1 cm
purchased 1997

**17** (p. 32)
Nigel Hall
(b. 1943, Bristol, UK)
*Untitled Drawing* 1972
charcoal on paper
56 x 76 cm
purchased 1972

**18** (p. 23)
Maggi Hambling
(b. 1945, Sudbury, UK)
*Drawing from Life:*
*Model in a Studio* 1966
pencil and gouache on paper collage
32.5 x 25 cm
purchased 1975

**19**
Maggi Hambling
*Tree 5* 1975
ink wash and charcoal on paper
39.2 x 28.7 cm
purchased 1975

**20** (p. 27)
Richard Hamilton
(b. 1922, London, UK)
*Swingeing London* 1968
charcoal, gouache and pencil on paper
34.5 x 45.5 cm
purchased 1969

**21** (p. 40)
Jane Harris (b. 1956, Swanage, UK)
*Untitled Drawing (3)* 1998-99
pencil on fabriano paper
55.5 x 76 cm
purchased 1999

**22** (p. 48)
David Hockney
(b. 1937, Bradford, UK)
*Fred and Marcia Weisman* 1968
oil pastel, ink and pencil on paper
35.5 x 42.9 cm
purchased 1972
© David Hockney

**23** (p. 19)
David Hockney
*French Shop* 1971
pencil on paper
43 x 35.2 cm
purchased 1972
© David Hockney

**24**
David Hockney
*The Island* 1971
pencil and crayon on paper
35.3 x 49.9 cm
purchased 1972

**25**
Tess Jaray
(b. 1937, Vienna, Austria)
*Untitled Working Drawing* 1981
pencil on graph paper
42 x 59.7 cm
purchased 1982

**26**
Allen Jones
(b. 1937, Southampton, UK)
*6 drawings for Falling Figure* 1964
crayon, watercolour and pencil
on paper
13.9 x 9.5 cm
purchased 1971

**27** (p. 20)
Allen Jones
*Sheet of drawings for Shoe Wheel*
1965-66
felt pen and pencil on paper
22.4 x 35.2 cm
purchased 1971

**28**
Emma Kay
(b.1961, London, UK)
*Map of the World from Memory*
*No.3* 1999
pencil on paper
145 x 242 cm
purchased 2000

**29**
Michael Kenny
(b. 1941, Liverpool, UK – d. 1999)
*The First Night* 1974
pencil and charcoal on paper
56 x 76.5 cm
purchased 1975

**30** (p. 45)
Michael Landy
(b. 1963, London, UK)
*Scrapheap Services* 1995
ink on paper
76 x 56 cm
purchased 1995

**31** (p. 17)
Bob Law
(b. 1934, Brentford, UK)
*Landscape Drawing, Wiltshire*
*Downs* 1966
pencil on paper
25.4 x 35.6 cm
purchased 1967

**32** (pp. 38–39)
Rachel Lowe
(b. 1968, Newcastle upon Tyne, UK)
*A Letter to an Unknown Person,*
*No. 5* 1998
Super 8 film transferred on to video
1.5 minutes
purchased 2001

**33** (p. 26)
L.S. Lowry
(b. 1887, Manchester, UK – d. 1976)
*Woman with Long Hair* 1964
pencil on paper
34.2 x 24.5 cm
purchased 1975
Reproduced by kind permission of
Miss Carol A. Lowry, the copyright owner

**34** (p. 42)
John Maxwell
(b. 1905, Dalbeattie, UK – d. 1962)
*Winter Bouquet* 1947
pen and ink on paper
55.9 x 45.7 cm
purchased 1947
© Estate of the artist 2001

**35** (p. 49)
Jim Medway
(b. 1974, Wakefield, UK)
*Shoe Shop* 1999
ballpoint pen and indian ink on paper
55 x 80 cm
purchased 1999

**36** (p. 18)
Edward Middleditch
(b. 1923, Chelmsford, UK – d. 1987)
*Bath c.*1953
black chalk and pencil on paper
28 x 40.5 cm
purchased 1954
© Estate of the artist 2001

**37**
Henry Moore
(b. 1898, Castleford, UK – d. 1986)
*Ideas for Sculpture: Transformation
of Bones* 1931
pencil on paper
22.9 x 19.7 cm
purchased 1963

**38**
Henry Moore
*Ideas for Sculpture: Transformation
of Bones* 1932
pencil on paper
22.9 x 19.7 cm
purchased 1963

**39** (p. 12)
Henry Moore
*Studies and Transformations of Bones
of Shells and Mushrooms* 1932
pencil on paper
24.8 x 17.1 cm
purchased 1963
Reproduced by permission of the
Henry Moore Foundadtion

**40** (p. 13)
Henry Moore
*Studies of Shells and Pebbles* 1932
pencil on paper
24.8 x 17.1 cm
purchased 1963
Reproduced by permission of the
Henry Moore Foundadtion

**41** (p. 16)
Ben Nicholson
(b. 1894, Denham, UK – d. 1982)
*Cloisters, San Gimignano* 1950
pencil on paper
38.1 x 50.8 cm
purchased 1954
© Angela Verren-Taunt 2001

**42**
Jacques Nimki
(b. 1959, Port Louis, Mauritius)
*Florilegium* 1998-99
graphite on paper
193 x 150.5 cm
purchased 1999

**43**
Viivi Oulasvirta
(b. 1930, Finland)
*Untitled* 1981
ink on paper
29.6 x 21 cm
purchased 1981

**44**
Eduardo Paolozzi
(b. 1924, Edinburgh, UK)
*Drawings from Rembrandt* 1945
pen and ink on paper
26.7 x 36.8 cm
purchased 1976

**45** (p. 44)
Eduardo Paolozzi
*Pitt-Rivers* 1945
ink and crayon on paper
38.1 x 56.5 cm
purchased 1976
© Eduardo Paolozzi 2001.
All Rights Reserved, DACS

**46** (p. 15)
Victor Pasmore
(b. 1908, Chelsham, UK – d. 1998)
*Beach in Cornwall* 1950
pen and ink on card
26 x 32.4 cm
purchased 1953
© Estate of the artist 2001

**47** (p. 43)
Simon Periton
(b. 1964, Faversham, UK)
*SP* 1995
blue foil paper
55.9 x 53.3 cm
purchased 1998

**48**
Deanna Petherbridge
(b. 1939, Pretoria, South Africa)
*Baoli II* 1980
pen and ink on paper
69.7 x 49.6 cm
purchased 1982

**49** (p. 31)
Carl Plackman
(b. 1943, Huddersfield, UK)
*Untitled Drawing ("Net")* 1969
pencil on paper
49.5 x 71.1 cm
purchased 1972

**50** (p. 21)
Bridget Riley
(b. 1931, London, UK)
*Structural and Tonal Movements in Opposition* 1966
pencil and gouache on graph paper
62.2 x 62.2 cm
purchased 1966

**51**
David Shrigley
(b. 1968, Glasgow, UK)
*'Take off...'* 1997
marker pen on paper
15 x 10 cm
purchased 1999

**52**
David Shrigley
*'These and others will be there to greet you at the airport...'* 1997
marker pen on paper
15 x 10 cm
purchased 1999

**53**
David Shrigley
*'At the earliest point of early morning...'* 1998
marker pen on paper
24 x 21 cm
purchased 1999

**54** (p. 52)
David Shrigley
*'Compare our prices against our competitors...'* 1998
marker pen on paper
24.5 x 26 cm
purchased 1999

**55** (p. 51)
David Shrigley
*'See the little creature in the giant cage...'* 1998
marker pen on paper
24 x 21 cm
purchased 1999

**56**
David Shrigley
*'The road to beasthood...'* 1998
marker pen on paper
24 x 20.5 cm
purchased 1999

**57**
Graham Sutherland
(b. 1903, London, UK)
*Drawing of a Palm Tree* 1948
pencil and watercolour on paper
22.2 x 17.1 cm
purchased 1954

**58**
William Tucker
(b. 1935, Cairo, Egypt)
*'T (Tunnel)' – Ti* 1975
pen and ink on paper
20.5 x 28.7 cm
purchased 1977

**59** (p. 25)
William Tucker
*'T (Tunnel)' – Tii* 1975
pen and ink on paper
20.5 x 28.7 cm
purchased 1977

**60**
William Tucker
*'T (Tunnel)' – Tiv* 1975
pen and ink on paper
20.5 x 28.7 cm
purchased 1977

**61**
William Tucker
*'T (Tunnel)' – Txii* 1975
pen and ink on paper
20.5 x 28.7 cm
purchased 1977

**62** (p. 41)
Keith Tyson
(b. 1969, Ulverston, UK)
*Applied Art Machine Chart: Candlestick Maker* 1999
mixed media on paper
157 x 126 cm
purchased 2000
© the artist, courtesy Anthony Reynolds Gallery, London

**63** (p. 22)
Euan Uglow
(b. 1932, London, UK – d. 2000)
*Figure in Profile* 1974
pencil on paper
30 x 24.5 cm
purchased 1975
© Estate of the artist 2001

**64** (p. 37)
Turi Werkner
(b. 1948, Innsbruck, Austria)
*MM33* 1976
pen and ink on transparent film
116.3 x 115.7 cm
purchased 1979